Instructor's Manual to Accompany

ACADEMIC WRITING

SECOND EDITION

Exploring Processes and Strategies

Ilona Leki

Manufactured in the United States of America.
9 8 7 6 5
f e d c b a

For information, write:
St. Martin's Press, Inc.
175 Fifth Avenue
New York, NY 10010

ISBN: 0-312-09215-6

Contents

I. COURSE SUGGESTIONS

Intended for students with TOEFL scores above 500, *Academic Writing: Exploring Processes and Strategies* contains fairly detailed explanations; it was intended for use both in the classroom as a guide for group activities and outside the classroom, almost like a programed text, as students work alone without the immediate guidance of their writing teacher. It helps students accomplish writing tasks by suggesting what to do first, how to proceed, how to solicit help, and how to decide when the task is finished. It calls for students to be actively engaged in analyzing what it is they do as they write because this engagement is expected to result in commitment to what they write. This commitment is important because while students can learn to write, in a sense, we cannot really teach writing. What we can do is to set up environments where writing is meaningful so that the students can discover what works best for them; we can respond to their writing so that they see the effect their writing has on others; and we can suggest options or strategies which we have seen to be successful for other students.

The many exercises and assignments in the text, more than most teachers will care to use in one term, are intended to provide the writing teacher with options from which to choose, particularly for subsequent terms. The material can be fairly thoroughly covered in a minimum of 15 weeks with 3 class meetings per week. The book can also be easily divided into two 10-week quarters with 3 class meetings per week. The writing assignments, including the Sequenced Writing Project, are given as possibilities. The Sequenced Writing Project consists of five different assignments on the same topic. About 25 writing assignments plus 4-6 possible essay exams comprise the selection to choose from. Each assignment is intended to focus on some particular feature of writing. For example, the survey focuses on extracting main ideas, the assignment on nonverbal communication on developing and supporting, the autobiography on editing. Peer response and self-analysis questions are all task specific.

Theoretical Bases

While not based strictly on any one theory of composing, this book takes a process approach to teaching writing, drawing on Britton's categories of informative writing and Kinneavy's aims of discourse for sequencing assignments. In taking this approach, the book makes several assumptions:

1. Students already know a great deal when they appear in our writing classes. These classes should allow them to move from current strengths toward new areas of skill and knowledge.

2. There is no single correct or most useful approach to a writing task. A writing class for novices should allow them to discover and use approaches that work well for *each of them.*

3. Since L2 writing is not the same as L1 writing, ESL writers need to be made consciously aware of the expectations of English-speaking readers in an academic setting.

4. Student writers should have the opportunity to practice a variety of types of writing including those typically required in higher education.

5. For the Sequenced Writing Project, a sequence of assignments on a single topic will allow students to develop the expertise in a subject to write with ease and confidence.

In light of these assumptions, the first part of the book helps the students develop a basic nonformulaic approach to writing tasks that call for information which the student already knows. Progressing toward more academic forms of writing, beginning in Chapter 5, students have the opportunity to describe, to narrate, and to use objective data in reporting simple analyses of information from the world around them.

The second half of the book focuses more directly on academic writing assignments, calling upon students to manipulate information obtained through reading and to incorporate it into their own projects, moving from analysis to synthesis to evaluation of that material.

All assignments suggested are ones that students have shown interest in and been successful at. Nevertheless, not all students will like every assignment. Some students are uncomfortable writing on subjects they consider personal; others relish expressing their opinions. For this reason, many of the assignments have two possible options, one more personal and one more objective.

Peer Responding and Self-Analysis

Nearly every assignment in this book has task-specific self-analysis and peer responding guide questions. These features are very important in helping to engage the student in the writing task. Peer responding allows students to learn from the ideas and from the language used by their classmates. It allows writers to have several readers, giving these writers a better sense of audience and purpose. It also builds students' confidence as they see they are being taken seriously both as writers and as readers. The purpose of the self-analysis questions is primarily to open a dialogue between the writer and the teacher. Students' answers to these questions can be extremely useful in helping the teacher see how the student conceived of the writing task and what that student's own sense was of success or failure in accomplishing it.

Students can read the questions for the Peer Responses and Self-Analyses in the book and write their answers on a separate sheet of paper. However, you may want to type up and distribute the Peer Response and Self-Analysis questions for each assignment. In this way you can see the questions and the students' answers all together. Also, by manipulating the amount of space you leave for each question, you can indicate the relative length of the responses you expect. Make sure to duplicate enough copies of the Peer Response guides so that each writer can get more than one response.

Peer responding is normally done in class. Students reading each other's papers sit together so that they can ask for clarifications from the writer if necessary. When the responder finishes, he/she gives the completed response sheet to the writer, who may then consult with the responder. The writer takes home all responses collected and considers them in preparing the second draft.

On the next day of class I collect the invention writing, the first draft, all the Peer Responses, the Self-Analysis sheet (which may be done after either the first or the second draft or both), and the second draft in order to see what kinds of decisions the writer made at these various points along the way. I make comments on all the Peer Response sheets and on all the Self-Analyses. The comments may be directed at either the original author or the peer responder, but since some students are more astute than others in responses to their peers and in their ability to analyze their own work, I make only encouraging or sympathizing comments on these sheets. Particularly as students are getting used to this system of responding, it is more important to give students confidence in their ability to read and respond than it is to get fully and correctly analyzed responses. When I return this batch of papers, I let the responders see all the comments I have made on the Peer Response sheets they filled out. They then return these sheets to the original author. In this way a kind of three-way dialogue is established among the writers, their responders, and the teacher.

Readings

The number of readings has been greatly expanded in this second edition. The readings are also intended to excite the students' interest, often raising controversial issues. But the readings are intended to enable writing. Thus, students should be encouraged to get ideas from the readings to use in their own writing as well as to argue with the readings whenever appropriate—in other words, to take from the content of the reading whatever may be useful to them in their thinking and writing rather than to consider the readings as part of a carefully constructed plan for reading instruction. Students should be encouraged to read for gist, guess meanings of words from context, and discuss the issues raised in the readings with each other. Although no glosses are provided, each reading is introduced with questions and commentary that should help activate appropriate form and content schemata for easier comprehension. The readings are loosely linked thematically to the writing assignments in the chapters in which they are assigned.

If the subject of a particular reading interests a student, suggestions for journal entries and further investigation are also provided at the end of each reading and at the end of this teacher's manual.

Responding/Evaluating/Grading

There is probably no aspect of higher education more antithetical to using a process approach to teaching writing than the requirement to grade student writing. Nevertheless, most of us are required to evaluate these products by giving grades. Some get around this contradiction by grading not the product but the students' success in manipulating the *process*. Others use a workshop approach, in which a minimal number of assignments must be completed to a minimal standard of acceptability, or a portfolio approach, in which instead of grading each paper during the term the teacher receives a student's portfolio of only three or four selected papers to evaluate at the end of the term.

While this text will work with any of these approaches, including the traditional one in which each paper receives a grade, research shows that the least helpful way to respond to a student's paper is to make elaborate commentary or grammatical corrections on a final draft. Teacher interventions in student writing, that is, comments which teachers make about a given paper, are most helpful when they come between drafts rather than on a final draft. One workable approach is to circulate among your students as they read and comment on each other's drafts during peer responding. You can quickly read through their drafts and discuss with the peer responder a section you question or a place where you want to propose an option. Making the suggestion to the peer responder and then having that student incorporate it into the peer response supports both the responder and the original writer. Another approach is to look at the Self-Analysis sheets during peer responding and to support or discourage changes the original writers themselves proposed.

While each assignment in this text calls for peer response followed by revision, not all papers need to be revised. On the other hand, a teacher or the writer may decide that more than one revision cycle may be appropriate for some papers. By the same token, not all papers need to be edited to perfection. The distance taken toward completion of any of these products should be determined by the teacher and/or the writer depending on what the goals of the course or the particular assignment may be. It is suggested, for example, that the autobiographical sketch be edited carefully since the student may want to use it in a real application.

II. CHAPTER COMMENTS AND SUGGESTIONS

Introduction

Here and throughout the book you might not want to have your students read all the explanatory material in the text; you may want simply to summarize it yourself for your students. Or better yet, since progress in writing comes from, among other things, reading, you may want to summarize the explanatory material first and then assign it to be read at home. Major instructional points are signaled throughout the text by a star in the margin. The style of the text was intended to sound like natural communication with students.

PART ONE: OVERVIEW OF WRITING PROCESSES

Chapter 1   Getting Started

Hints

It is a good idea to go over, as a class, the writing hints listed here, adding whatever commentary you feel necessary. The hints reappear individually in chapters that elaborate on or give practice implementing them.

Writing Assignment 1.1: Sample

Most teachers like to get a writing sample at the beginning of a term to have an idea of where their students are in their development as writers and L2 users. The students will return to the paper they write here after they learn different methods of invention. The self-analysis questions and the questions for class discussion are intended to get the students used to analyzing their writing and to make them consciously consider their current writing processes.

Overviews

To give students an idea of what their task will be throughout the term, the section called Overview of Writing Processes proposes a writing assignment similar to one that might appear in a history course. Students are guided through this assignment and assured that they will receive further, more detailed instruction on the different subsections of writing tasks as the term progresses.

The topic selected for this simulated history assignment, based on a reading from *Bury My Heart at Wounded Knee*, is potentially controversial. While such a topic would not be unusual in a college-level course, if you prefer a less controversial topic, an alternative subject and supporting material are available at the end of Appendix A.

The section entitled Overview of This Book is intended to allow both students and teachers a sense of what this more detailed instruction will entail. Also at the beginning of each major division of the book, a schematic diagram of the book appears to enable students and teachers to see where they are at that point in relation to the rest of the text.

PART TWO: WRITING FROM OBSERVATION AND EXPERIENCE

UNIT ONE: GETTING TO DRAFT ONE

Chapter 2 Getting Ideas and Starting to Write

Journals

Journal suggestions appear in this section on keeping journals, throughout the chapters, and at the end of each reading. In each case the suggested topics are loosely related to the theme of the chapter or reading. Students are to make three entries per week although there may be more than three suggestions to choose from in a given chapter. Students should feel free to go back to suggestions they are interested in but did not write on earlier. The teacher's manual also contains additional journal suggestions that you may want to type up and provide to your students.

Most students enjoy thinking about and answering the questions in the Journal Suggestions but sometimes have one of two complaints: that it takes too long to write journal entries and that their teacher does not correct their grammar. In answer to the first complaint, you might point out that since these journals are intended to develop fluency three 15-minute periods are a minimum to help student writers feel comfortable writing. You may occasionally (or even for all three 15-minute periods if you have the time available) give your students time in class to write their journal entries. In answer to the second complaint, students sometimes need to be convinced that while grammatical accuracy is important in some kinds of writing, fluency, not correctness, is being developed here. In these journals students should feel free to experiment with their English.

Journals can be collected once a week and checked for number and length of entries. Some colleagues of mine, maintaining that students benefit merely through the process of writing the journal, never even read what the student writes. I have found their entries so fascinating, however, that I look forward to reading the journal each week, occasionally making brief comments as a simple interested reader.

As you look at the sample journal entries in this chapter, I suggest you discuss what your students liked and/or noticed about them and then decide as a class whether or not your journals will be private. If you decide to make them public, you may want to gather excerpts from the journals or summarize the more interesting entries once a week, type them up, and distribute them. Student are usually proud and pleased to see their entries distributed to classmates.

Invention

Teaching and practicing all the invention strategies takes quite a while, probably 3-4 class hours. To make sure students see how to get maximum benefit from the various invention options, it is a good idea for you to look quickly over the invention practices that your students do here or to have classmates look at each other's inventions in groups.

Cubing calls for students to look at an idea from six different angles, any of which could prove to be a fruitful way to develop thoughts on the initial idea. These "sides" or angles also parallel several of the traditional rhetorical modes. Thus, this heuristic can be used to approach teaching rhetorical modes if you wish: describe, narrate (associate), compare/contrast, and divide/classify.

Additional Journal Suggestions for Writing Assignment 2.2

—Are there legends in your culture about great heroes who probably never existed? Describe one of them. What did he or she do? Was this hero human or not? What kinds of qualities did this hero have that people in your culture admire? What stories do they tell about this hero?
—Describe three things from your culture that a stranger to your country would have difficulty understanding. (Don't pick something like language.)
—What kinds of misconceptions do Americans (or anyone in the world) have about your country? What kinds of misconceptions do Americans have about any foreigners?
—Do you have an Independence Day or a national holiday? Explain what it is you celebrate, when independence occurred, under what circumstances it occurred, and what changes occurred after independence. What do you do to celebrate this day?
—What is the nature of marriage in your country? Is it a contract

with duties, obligations, and rights? Is it an emotional proof of love? At what age do most people seem to marry? Are marriages still arranged in your country by the couples' parents? How successful do these marriages seem to be? How is divorce viewed in your culture? Can either the husband or the wife initiate divorce proceedings? What kinds of grounds are legitimate reasons for divorce? How do you feel about divorce?

Writing Assignment 2.2

The assignment on an artifact or tradition from your students' cultures will be referred to several times in the first four chapters of this book. If you choose to have your students do this assignment, encourage them to keep trying different invention strategies with this same project, not to get it better necessarily but just so that they can see that there are many options in approaching a topic to write on. This is an exploration of their own writing processes. On subsequent assignments your students can take short cuts, using only strategies that work well for them and taking the material they write through however many revisions they or you feel they need.

At this point you may decide that you would like your students to complete a full draft of one of the assignments suggested here. If so, you may want to direct your students to the instructions on drafting in Chapter 4 now and come back to Chapter 3 later.

Sequenced Writing Project

The third possible assignment described in this chapter begins a series of five sequenced assignments. This project has the advantage of allowing students to build on their growing knowledge of the topic they choose, as they complete each step of the series, creating self-confidence in the writer and often making for fascinating reading. Students have written successfully on typically disastrous topics such as abortion, drugs, and air pollution. However, topic selection is crucially tied to each of the three requirements listed in the students' texts. If all three requirements are not fully met, students have seemed unable to sustain interest in the project for the whole series of five papers. This fading interest is a potential problem even if the topic selection requirements are met. On the other hand, when the project works as planned, which has been most of the time, both the writers themselves and their teachers come away quite impressed with the results.

Chapter 3 Preparing for a Draft

Audience

In most cases the real audience for your writing students will be you and the rest of the class, certainly a legitimate audience. If your students can grasp the idea that writing for an audience can <u>help</u> them make decisions about ideas, organization, vocabulary, etc., their writing tasks will be much easier. On the other hand, it is worth pointing out to them that sometimes the idea of some particular audience can also intimidate writers. If this occurs and causes your students to block, in order to get their ideas flowing again, they should forget the audience and write only for themselves until they have discovered or reconnected with the ideas they want to express; they can then reconjure up the thought of that particular audience and reorganize or edit what they have written.

Exercise 3: Making McDonald's ads to appeal to different audiences

If your students are not familiar enough with McDonald's to do this assignment, pick any restaurant in your area which they are likely to be familiar with and that might try to appeal to a variety of customers.

Additional Journal Suggestions

—Look through magazine ads for a few minutes. What kinds of things are advertised most? What does this suggest to you about U.S. culture? What kinds of appeals are the advertisers making? That is, what are they trying to appeal to in their audience? From looking at the ads, who do you feel is the advertisers' audience? How old are they? How wealthy are they? What other assumptions did the advertisers make about their audience?
—For the next couple of days pay attention to bits of conversation you happen to overhear. Just from what you overhear, try to create a history for these people. Who are they? What do they do? What are they like? Invent anything your imagination suggests.

Chapter 4   Writing a First Draft and Getting Feedback

Writing Assignment 4.1

You may want your students to do more than one of these, working through this section with one and then again with another writing assignment.

Whether drafts should be written at home or in class depends on a number of variables, including time available. However, in most real life writing situations and even in most academic writing situations (except for exams) writing is done outside class when the writer finally feels ready. Some writing teachers understandably contend that writing in class helps build the discipline required to write, makes the writing assignment seem particularly important since class time is devoted to it, and allows student to ask the teacher questions as the questions occur. Others feel that students should be allowed to write wherever and whenever they feel ready, just as more experienced writers do. Whichever writing situation you choose, your students should also be encouraged to take their time with the pre- and post-draft Self-Analysis. So that the students see the Self-Analysis as important not only for the development of their skills in analyzing their own writing but also as an important means of communicating with their teacher, the Self-Analysis should be collected with any draft you look at. Your comments on the Self-Analysis can be quite brief, but I suggest looking for places where your comments can support or complement what the student has written rather than contradict it.

Getting Feedback

The three student examples were chosen because most writing teachers would see the one on nonverbal communication as clearly the best. It is important, however, that students understand that each of these short drafts have good qualities and are basically perfectly acceptable *early* drafts. The weakest one is probably the one on the pleasures of high school, but even in that one the student attempted to be specific by naming her classmates and trying to give neatly organized examples of good features of her school. It would not be a good idea to let students become too critical (as they are sometimes prone to be with other students' writing) of any of these examples because in this chapter they will share their writing with their classmates, exposing their egos. It is important that they feel as confident as possible that their attempts will be well received. Otherwise, they will not be able to participate in or benefit fully from the peer responding they will do.

The second purpose of this exercise beyond giving students practice in responding together to student writing is to allow them to see the criteria by which you, their teacher, judge student writing. What you have to say about each of these pieces will determine to a great extent what your students will try to provide in the papers they write for your class. Rather than criticizing any weaknesses in these papers, look for good features in each of them and point out that these are the features you will look for in their writing.

UNIT TWO: WORKING WITH A DRAFT

Chapter 5   Focusing on Main Ideas

Main Ideas

The following dictation exercise may further help students focus on the movement from general to specific. Have your students take out two sheets of paper. As you dictate the following short article, stop at each marked point in the text. On the first sheet of paper, have the students write down what you dictate. On the second sheet, have them write down their guesses about what the next sentence will be. Have the students compare their guesses and try to explain what prompted them to guess as they did. Ask them what the clues were in the previously dictated material which led them to their hypotheses.

Or, instead of having the students write their predictions down on the second sheet of paper, you may simply want to discuss what directions they think the text will move.

> Although all human beings measure time, there are wide variations in how different cultures understand time. # For example, what is considered late in one culture may not be in another. # The story of an American professor teaching in Brazil illustrates this point. His class was scheduled to begin at 10 o'clock. # But when he arrived at 10, the class was nearly empty. The students arrived some time between 10 and 11:15. # They did not feel that they were arriving late. On the other hand, # the class was scheduled to end at 12. # Therefore, the American professor finished his lecture promptly at 12 and prepared to leave. # But the Brazilian students remained for as long as an hour asking questions. The American expected class to begin promptly at 10 and to end at 12. # The Brazilians were much less concerned about what the clock was telling them to do. # Thus, while people share the concept of time, the particulars of what time means and how we conceive of it are very different.

Diagram of academic essay

The diagram of a typical academic essay is provided because some students profit by seeing schematic representations. While the diagram in general terms accurately represents one way to structure academic essays, students should not get the impression that they must select and develop only ideas which fit this very general form.

Writing Assignment 5.2

Students usually enjoy this assignment. You may want to begin by referring students to the explanation of the writing assignment at the end of the chapter so that they can be thinking about gathering data well before the first draft of the report is due. Working in groups of two or three and reporting results orally to the class have both worked well with this assignment.

—Have you ever responded to some news or to an incident in a way that surprised you, either in a way that embarrassed you and made you feel ashamed or in a way that you were proud of? Analyze your response. Why did you react the way you did? What do you think caused that particular, unusual response at that particular time?

—Write down in your language all the sayings you can think of and then translate them into English. Which ones seem the truest to you? Can you think of an incident that proves the wisdom of one of the sayings?

—Tell the story of one of your most embarrassing (or sad or exciting) moments. Why do you think this incident is important to you?

—Do you have any unreasonable fears? Can you give the cause, the root of one of these fears? What effect has it had on your life?

—When do you first remember realizing that you loved something or someone? What made you realize you loved that person or thing? A joyful feeling or a painful feeling?

—What are the characteristics in your culture of the perfect husband, wife, child? What would/do you look for in a partner? What do you hope your child will be like as a child? As an adult?

—A proverb in English states: When in Rome, do as the Romans do. Suppose you find yourself at a nude beach. Do you undress too? Or suppose you have to use the bathroom, and there is none in sight. What do you do? Or suppose that in your country you were taught not to throw gum or candy wrappers or other garbage on the street but you are in a country where you see others doing that. Do you begin to do it too?

—What kinds of behavior are completely accepted or absolutely rejected by society in a relationship between an unmarried male and female at various ages? before adolescence, in high school, in college, in their 20s, in their 40s, in their 60s?

—What did you imagine college would be like before you started classes? How did the actual experience differ from your anticipation?

—Which of your country's customs or holidays have the most meaning for you? Why?

Chapter 6   Developing and Shaping Ideas

Development

Since the writing assignments in this chapter call for invention activities which may take some time, these activities are described at the beginning of the chapter so that students may get started well before the first draft is due.

Additional Journal Suggestions

—What actions are permitted to women in your country but not to men and the other way around? Are men allowed to cry without shame? Women? Would it be considered unusual for men to kiss or hold hands in the street? For women? Are men allowed to go to certain places where women normally are not allowed? How can you explain these differences? Do you approve of them or not?

—Think of *one* example of nonverbal communication in your country that could be misinterpreted here and *one* example of nonverbal communication here that could be misinterpreted in your country. Consider perceptions of time and space too.

—What kinds of things do you do and not do to someone who for one reason or another you consider a superior or to whom you must show respect? To someone who you consider a subordinate or from whom you expect to get respect? What do you call them? How do you look at them?

—What do you associate with Monday morning, Sunday morning, Saturday night, Friday night, or any other time of the week now that you live in the United States? What did you used to associate with this time while you lived at home? Fill in the following blanks with lists or sentences. Try to include details of sight, sound, smell, feeling, and taste.

> Sunday morning (or whatever time you chose) is (or was) . . .
> It is (or was) a time to . . .
> It is (or was) like . . .

—What is your first memory? How old were you? Describe everything you remember.

—If you have a picture from back home that you like very much, look at that picture. Describe what everything looks like and what people are doing. Who is there? Where is it? What day is it? What time of day is it? What is the weather like? What has just happened? What is about to happen? (You don't have to answer each question; just think about it and answer the ones that give interesting details.) What colors are associated in your mind with these scenes, what objects, what clothes? Try to find details for all the senses.

Using specifics

As students answer the questions on specific descriptions of an embarrassed person, an angry person, and a good class atmosphere, keep pushing them to be more specific. For example, if students say that a red face indicates embarrassment and then say that a red face also indicates anger, push them to specify how one can tell the difference between an embarrassed red face and an angry one. Or if students

13

say that attentive students are signs of a good atmosphere in class, ask what attentive students look like.

The student writing sample about distances Chinese maintain in conversation calls for students to analyze the relative specificity of each sentence in the short test. The answers are (S = sentence):

Most general: S1_____S7
More specific: ___S2_____S5_____
Most specific: _____S3____S4_____S6____

The exercise is intended to illustrate graphically how texts move back and forth between general and specific statements.

Writing Assignment 6.1

In the explanation of the writing assignment on nonverbal communication a number of questions are raised about audience, main ideas, development, and organization. Since they are fairly detailed, students may want to refer to these questions as they prepare for later writing assignments also.

Chapter 7 Beginning and Ending Drafts

The diagram of an essay presented here is the traditional one. Again some students react well to diagrams, and for those students this diagram may clarify how essays can be set up. Obviously, not all essays follow this pattern; the diagram should not be thought of as a formula for good essays.

Additional Journal Suggestions

—How do you feel about using extraordinary means to keep people alive who are dying? Should these means be used for anyone or only for young people? Who should decide whether a person should be allowed to die naturally or be kept alive artificially?

—Animals are used in experiments of all kinds, from testing chemicals used in cosmetics to research in AIDS. Which animals should be used in these experiments? What limits should there be, if any, on using animals for experiments that scientists claim will make human life better?

—Should children be exposed to as many experiences as possible to help them learn to cope earlier with the harsh realities of life or should they be protected from ugliness as long as possible? How would a child who was brought up in the first way behave? And the second? What kind of adults might they become?

—Would you yourself rather see/know everything—good and bad—about life or would you rather be protected from knowing about the bad things if they were never going to touch your life? If you had an incurable disease, would you want to know about it? If someone you loved had an incurable disease, would you want him or her to know about it? Would you tell the person?

UNIT THREE: REWORKING THE DRAFT

Chapter 8   Revising

You have perhaps asked your students to revise the work they have been doing all term, but in this section students see some specific revision strategies with both problems and possible solutions and two actual student examples. Students may want to look briefly over the problems/solutions list and mark that section for future reference. The two student examples should be analyzed together in class.

The writing assignment in this chapter calls for revision of a previously written assignment. Even if your students are satisfied with all their previously written assignments, encourage them, if only for this assignment, to practice revising as it is discussed in this chapter so that they will see that it is always possible to change what they have written.

As with the questions for the writing assignment on nonverbal communication in Chapter 6 and the revision problems and solutions strategies list in this chapter, student may want to mark for future reference the questions on the revision assignment at the end of this chapter.

Additional Journal Suggestions

—What aspects of student life in the United States do you not enjoy? What do you enjoy? How is the life of a student in your country different from what it is here?
—Have your attitudes toward the United States or toward your own country changed since you began living here? What do you now see differently from before? Or are your attitudes basically the same but intensified?
—During the time you have been in this country, who has become important in your life? Who have you become important to in the United States? What good have you done them or they you? What has gotten you in trouble since you have been here?
—Have you noticed any difference between what is considered good writing style in the United States and what is considered good writ-

ing style in your language? What are those differences? What constitutes good writing in your language?

Chapter 9   Polishing Revised Drafts

Rephrasing

Inexperienced writers, especially if they are not writing in their own language, sometimes forget that any idea can be expressed in a number of ways. Once they have written a sentence, they sometimes feel excessively committed to it (preferring, as others have said about the reluctance to revise, any written version of an idea however unsatisfactory to the chaos of trying to get the idea into words). In the rephrasing exercise at the beginning of this chapter, students have the opportunity to see many different ways of expressing the same idea. Some of the class's suggestions will be better than others, but the point here is for the students to demonstrate to themselves that they *can* come up with alternative ways to express any idea.

Please point out to your students that the short sample text by Keihan Mani was simplified for the exercise on sentence combining.

Editing

Please point out that the errors in Exercises 7 and 8 were added to the original text. Some of the errors are quite obvious and "serious," others are not, but all are typical errors of advanced ESL writers.

Additional Journal Suggestions

—What are you most looking forward to in the short run? In the long run?
—What mistakes have you made in the past which you will probably make again? Which will you never make again?
—What kinds of self-improvement or New Year's resolutions have you ever made? Which did you stick to, which did you abandon? Why, in each case? Can you see a pattern in your successes and failures to stick to your resolutions?
—Are there parts of your personality you would like to change? Do you sometimes do things you don't want to do but can't stop yourself from doing? What is there about yourself you would like to be able to control better?
—Think of the compulsions you have. Do you smoke? Have you ever tried to stop? With what success? Are there other things you feel compelled to do even when you don't want to or know you shouldn't? Do you work too much? Sleep too much? Watch too much television? Eat too much? Why do you think people have compulsions like these?

—Think of what you were told as a child about life, people, the world, or anything else that later turned out not to be true. What were you told and what did you realize later?
—What kind of men/women are you attracted to or do you go out with? What similarities do you find in the friends you make? Are your friends mostly similar to each other in age, education, background, and interests or do you have friends who are quite different from each other? Do you have certain kinds of friends for certain occasions? Explain.
—What kinds of Americans have you met since you came here? What kinds of students have you met here from your own country? Are they the same types you would have met at a university at home or are they different types?
—Think of what you were like at age 13. What were your concerns? What opinions did you hold strongly? What did you like to do? How have you changed since that time? How have your concerns, opinions, and interests changed?

Writing Assignment 9.2

You may find it convenient to duplicate the sample autobiography that your students are to reduce from 550 to 300 words. If your students do their editing on the duplicated sheets, you can check their reductions more easily.

Additional writing assignment

Get together in groups of four or five and together create an imaginary job description like the samples below. Assume that these jobs are meant to be for people just finishing college. Try to think of jobs that you and your classmates might actually be qualified for eventually, emphasizing personal qualities that would be important in the job.

—Wanted: Computer program de-bugger, willingness to work in a team, ability to tactfully suggest changes to colleagues, ability to find imaginative solutions to problems as they occur, no fixed duties beyond trouble-shooting, applicant must be persistent and imaginative. $29,000.
—Wanted: Accountant, working with figures, ability to work alone, steadily, and regularly at the same task every day, job demands great accuracy, work with details. $25,000.
—Wanted: International Student Advisor, time abroad, interest in students, ability to get along with administrators, willingness to spend off-work hours with students, willingness to be on call for emergencies, rewards more personal than monetary. $20,000.

After your group has written the job description, give it to another group. When your group receives the job description, each of you will write a short autobiographical sketch as part of an imaginary job application, emphasizing your qualities that fit this job. Write your sketch as though you were just finishing college with a degree in the field advertised in this description. However, refer to your real qualities, not imaginary ones, and any pertinent, real experiences you may have had that would fit the job description. When your group finishes, give all your autobiographical sketches to the group that wrote the job description. When you get your group of autobiographical sketches, as a group read each one and select the best person for the job you created and list the reasons for your choice.

PART THREE: APPLYING WRITING PROCESSES FOR ACADEMIC PURPOSES

UNIT FOUR: USING PUBLISHED SOURCES

Chapter 10   Summarizing, Paraphrasing, and Quoting Sources

The sample summaries to be analyzed all have both good and bad features. Summary 1 begins by properly citing the title and author of the article, but sentence 2 of the summary editorializes. The third sentence uses words directly from the original. But the summary does a good job of correctly interpreting and focusing on the major points of the original. In Summary 2 the author and the title of the article are not mentioned at the beginning as they should be, and the summary contains too much detail (the name and affiliation of the doctor; the number of cups of coffee needed to produce side effects). The main idea is interpreted correctly, however. Although Summary 3 cites the author and title of the article correctly, the first and third sentences contain inappropriate editorial comments with misinformation (that everyone needs 7-9 hours of sleep). The rest of the summary correctly interprets the original until the last sentence, which again editorializes.

Sequenced Writing Project

While the summaries themselves may not present much of a problem at this point, linking the three summaries together in a coherent paper is more challenging and may require increased teacher intervention throughout the writing process.

Chapter 11   Documenting Sources

The short section on documentation is intended as a reference for students rather than as information that they should memorize. On the other hand, it is useful for students to have a general idea in their heads about what sort of information must be included to correctly cite a source even if they cannot remember whether periods or commas separate the sections of a citation. The style used here is the simplified MLA style but students should be reminded that different disciplines use different styles and that they should check with content area teachers to determine if the style given here is acceptable.

UNIT FIVE: ACADEMIC WRITING TASKS

Chapter 12   Analyzing Issues

Although all the writing assignments in Chapters 12, 13, and 14 are representative of academic writing tasks, you may wish to select from among them rather than to assign them all. Many academic writing assignments call for some analysis and/or synthesis of ideas found in reading. Similar approaches are required in the writing assignments in Chapters 13 and 14. Chapter 13 and the first writing assignment in Chapter 14 provide the texts the students are to work from; in the second writing assignment in Chapter 14, students find their own written sources, a much more difficult and time-consuming task.

The writing assignments in these three chapters on academic writing tasks are all intended to help students develop an academic approach to writing by calling upon them to analyze situations and events. The first assignment requires students to look objectively at both sides of an issue raised by their own educational experiences. Sometimes this assignment causes students to recall and relate some very negative experiences they had in primary or secondary school, but asking about the pros/cons or advantages/disadvantages of a situation is a common academic writing assignment. This assignment is intended to push students toward adopting an approach that looks calmly at both sides of issues. The assignments on explaining a problem and proposing a solution also reflect academic writing assignments in content courses. In these assignments students are again asked to maintain a reasonable and detached stance as they analyze problems and propose solutions.

If your students are doing the Sequenced Writing Project, there are two options for the project's final report. The first appears in Chapter 12; the second comes in Chapter 14. It seems most reasonable to assign one or the other but not both for fear of having students become tired of their topic.

Additional Journal Suggestions

—Are children getting younger in your society? That is, do they start doing adult things (smoking, going out) earlier than they did when you were a child? What other changes have you been able to notice about children's behavior between the time you were a child and now? If you have younger siblings, do they do things you were not permitted to do at that age? On the other hand, if you have older siblings, do you do things, or as a child did you do things, they didn't do at the same age?

—Is it good to be the only child in a family or to have siblings? What are the advantages and disadvantages of each? If you have children, ideally will you want one or more? Why?

—Are oldest or youngest children in a family treated differently in your culture? Does the oldest, for example, have duties and/or privileges that the youngest does not have even when he/she gets to be the same age?

—What are you most proud of your country for doing? What are you most ashamed of it for doing? What values in your culture are you most proud of?

—Write an assessment of your progress in English up to now. What can you now do quite well and easily in English? What still gives you trouble? How can you solve your problems with English?

—Think about your progress in this course. How do you feel about what you have been doing here? Are there things you don't like? What would you like changed? How would you propose to change what you don't like? What do you enjoy about the course so far? Do you feel you have made progress in writing in English? What do you feel you still need to work on in order to become an even better writer? How can this class help you do so better?

Chapter 13   Responding to Written Assignments

The entire chapter is devoted to a detailed analysis of two opposing arguments. It draws, therefore, on the writing assignments in Chapter 12 (analyzing the pros and cons of an issue, analyzing a problem, and using the analysis to move toward suggesting a solution). In addition, analysis of these arguments serves as an introduction to Chapter 14 in which students construct arguments.

Here, after a careful analysis of the positions taken by the two authors, students construct a limited response, restricted to only one or two propositions. Many students come from educational systems that do separate gifted children from regular children, and in fact, many ESL students studying in the United States were once these very same gifted children. Discussion of the issues raised by the article is usually lively, and students have clear positions they want to take and examples from their own lives they want to use as evidence to support the positions they take in their papers. They should be encouraged to cite the two authors here in their papers as well.

—What should/do schools teach besides academic subjects? Should trades be taught as well or should young people learn trades as apprentices? What kinds of schools are there in your country?

—In your own family, was education always highly prized? Was it taken for granted that you would go to college? Did you yourself always want a college education and assume you would get one?

—What problems or advantages do you think confront people who are naturally extremely intelligent, geniuses? How do they relate to average people? How do you think they handle any problems that arise? What about very beautiful people? Do you think that their beauty might cause problems for them in their relationships with other people? What kinds? Why?

Chapter 14   Arguing from Written Material

Constructing an argument is a difficult rhetorical skill, some say too difficult for young college students to handle, particular when these students are likely to be relatively inexpert about most subjects on which they might take a position. As a result, they have only a weak sense of what constitutes proof in a given argument in a given field. The two writing assignments in this chapter are, nevertheless, proposed for those teachers who feel that students should at least be exposed to persuasive writing or argumentation, even in a beginning college level writing course.

Writing Assignment 14.1

In this writing assignment, encourage students to use information from all four of the sources, if possible, in support of whatever position they decide to argue.

Writing Assignment 14.2

An argument of the type referred to in this section (especially the sample subjects students have chosen to write on in the past) is difficult. But students enjoy having the opportunity to write about a subject currently controversial and being discussed in the news and among friends. They seem to feel empowered when their assignment in English class directs them toward becoming well informed on one of these issues. However, if you feel that the subjects of the type students have selected in the past are too broad and perhaps too controversial, your students might be directed toward more local issues at your school or in the community.

In either case, it has proven well worth the time spent to have the students do a 5-10 minute report to the rest of the class on the subjects they choose. If the report is presented before the final draft is written, the writers can benefit from the questions or points made by classmates and can consider incorporating these comments into the final draft.

The writing assignment instructs students to duplicate the pages of any publications they use and to underline the sections they used. The point of this instruction is to allow teachers to check sources and accuracy of citations.

Additional Journal Suggestions

—Should people get respect even if they don't deserve it just because of the positions they hold in our society? Think of parents, teachers, politicians, etc. If you think these people deserve respect because of their positions, why do you think so? If not, when should people get respect from others? Which people? Old people? Why? Who else? Why?

—What is considered proper classroom behavior in your country? What do *you* consider proper classroom behavior? If you could set the rules, what rules would you set and how would you defend your decisions?

—To what extent does anyone have the right to control your private behavior? If you are doing something self-destructive, who has the right to stop you? Society? Government? Employers? Parents? Friends?

—Do you feel that somewhere in the world the perfect mate for you is living? How do people go about finding and then proving to themselves that they have found the perfect mate? What is the best way to know whether someone is suitable as a mate for you? Should you rely on the opinions of your family and friends to help you decide on a mate or only on your own feelings? What advice would you give a child of yours about looking for a mate? Is it really necessary to have a mate in the first place?

—Is it important to be in love with the person you marry? Why? Is it important to stay married even if you no longer feel in love? What can you do to stay in love with another person or to keep another person in love with you?

—If you were suddenly given the right to dictate the behavior of people around you, what would you forbid and what would you force people to do?

—Some Americans have a nostalgia for a less mechanized, simpler, more natural way of life: no machines, no cars, homemade bread, home-grown vegetables, farm animals for milk, cheese, meat. Do many people in your country regret technological advances or not? Do you? Comment on the American nostalgia for the simpler way of life.

Chapter 15 Preparing for an Essay Exam

Encourage your students to try to come up with actual essay exam questions for a course they are taking or to recall questions they have had to answer in previous courses. If any of them happen to be enrolled in a course in which you yourself might be qualified to ask essay exam questions, construct a few you feel would be appropriate for that course and discuss them with your class, explaining why you asked those particular questions and what you would be looking for in an answer.

Chapter 16 Practicing Taking Essay Exams

The four sections of this chapter focus on organizational strategies that might be called upon in typical essay exam questions. The strategies are not all-inclusive, but they are common. Students can save themselves a good deal of time if they can recognize that an exam question is calling for a particular organizational strategy in the response. These four sections are intended to give students practice in answering some commonly phrased questions.

In addition to (or in place of) the suggested readings and simulated essay exam questions presented here, teachers may want to draw upon the Mott and Bettelheim articles from Chapter 13 for practice exam questions. Some possible exam questions might be:

1. Mott bases his argument that gifted children should not be in the same classes as ordinary children on a particular definition of gifted children. How does Mott define gifted and how does that definition fit into his argument for separated classes?

2. Bettelheim believes in the positive results of mixing students of various abilities in the same class. What are some of the positive results he mentions?

3. Both Mott and Bettelheim discuss the results of experiments with grouping or mixing gifted children and ordinary children. Compare the two experiments and the results of each one.

4. Bettelheim refers to several negative results of grouping gifted children. Describe these results and how they come about.

5. Mott refers to the frustration of children in mixed classes. Which children are frustrated and why? Compare this explanation with that of Bettelheim on the same subject.

Whether students respond to sample exam questions from the Mott and Bettelheim articles or from the suggested readings, they should follow the same procedure set up in Chapter 16 of trying to guess what questions might be asked, inventing, writing for 20 minutes, answering the Self-Analysis questions, and then exchanging papers with a classmate.

If these essay exams are going to be graded to give students an idea of how successfully they responded to the essay exam questions, the best approach is probably to grade the papers as though they were in fact essay exams rather than final drafts of essays. It is also a good idea to discuss with your students the criteria you intend to use in evaluating these essay exams.

III APPENDIX A: READINGS

Bury My Heart at Wounded Knee

Additional Journal Suggestions

—Are there (or were there) groups of people in your country who have historically been left out of the mainstream? Why were they left out? Where do they live? How do they govern themselves? How do they survive economically?

Research Suggestion

If you are interested in the subject of Native Americans, including Eskimos and Polynesians, do library research to find more information on them. Since there are so many different tribes, you may want to choose one from the part of the country where you are now living. You may be interested in discovering how marriages were decided upon, what the role of the medicine man was, how religion affected daily lives, how these people viewed themselves in relation to nature, how your tribe first reacted to European/white people, how they reacted to the infamous cruelty and injustice they suffered at the hands of these invaders of their land, and how and where your tribe is living now. Or you may want to look into the life of one of the many great Indian leaders, such as Geronimo, Sitting Bull, Tecumseh, Osceola, or Chief Joseph.

Do Not Disturb

Additional Journal Suggestion

—What are the creation myths in your culture? What traditional beliefs have you heard about how the earth was formed and how human beings came to be?

Taking the Bungee Plunge

Additional Journal Suggestion

—Do people gamble much in your culture? How are gamblers viewed? What kind of gambling do people do?

Black Holes and Baby Universes

Research Suggestion

—If you are interested in cosmology or the study of the universe, look for more information on it at the library. You might explore the following ideas or create questions of your own.

What is a black hole in space?
What causes the Northern Lights, the Aurora Borealis?
What are novas and supernovas?
What is the difference between comets and meteors?
What folk beliefs explain comets, meteors, or eclipses?

The First Four Minutes

Additional Journal Suggestions

—What kind of image of yourself do you like to portray when you meet someone? Do you feel you are usually successful at portraying yourself as you want to be seen? Is the personality you use when you first meet someone the real you?

—It is said that people like people who like themselves. How do people act who like themselves? How do they show they like themselves? How do people behave who don't like themselves?

Research Suggestion

If you are interested in the topic of this reading, look for Leonard Zunin's book, *Contact: The First Four Minutes*, at the library and find out more about this subject.

Nonverbal Communication

Research Suggestion

If you are interested in the subject of nonverbal communication, do some research to find out more about it. You might include research on animal communication as well. What kinds of things do animals communicate to each other and how do they do it?

Abraham Lincoln

Additional Journal Suggestions

—Certain characters in history have very negative or very positive reputations. Do you know of such villains or heroes in your country? Write about one or more of them. Who were they? What did they do? Is their bad or good reputation justified in your opinion? How does their good or bad reputation reflect basic values in your culture? In the United States, for example, the fact that Lincoln came from a poor background, educated himself, and was eventually elected president fits into the popular American myth that everyone in the United States has an equal chance to become great even if they begin small. Do people still point to your country's heroes as models for present-day behavior?

—Who is more likely to be a successful leader—a person who comes from the people or a person who was raised in wealth? What would you imagine the differences would be between these two types in terms of loyalties, moral strength, education, political and social connections and obligations, political outlook, economic preferences, or anything else you can think of?

Research Suggestion

If you are interested in Abraham Lincoln, do some library research and find out more about him. Areas to explore might be: his relationship with his wife, Mary Todd; accounts of his personality; his feelings about slavery before the Civil War; his death; the reaction of the country, both North and South, to his death; what might have happened if Lincoln had not been murdered; John Wilkes Booth, Lincoln's assassin—what kind of person was he? What finally happened to him?

Who Are Smarter—Boys or Girls?

Additional Journal Suggestions

—Are little girls and boys treated differently in your society? in your family? Is this as it should be or not? Why? What advantages or disadvantages are there to treating someone a certain way only because of their sex?

—Would you rather be a male or a female in your society? Whose life is better? What are the advantages and disadvantages of each one? Do you think more men would want to be women or to live women's lives or more women would want to be men or lead men's lives? Why?

Research Suggestion

If you are interested in the subject of this reading, find out more about the subtle way we train baby girls and baby boys to behave differently as adults. You might look for information on how infants are treated differently from the day of their birth depending on their sex. Look for information on how teachers also subtly discourage little girls and encourage little boys in school. Finally, see what you can notice even at the university level or among educated people about how our society discourages females and males from developing in certain directions.

A View from Other Cultures: Must Men Fear "Women's Work"?

Additional Journal Suggestion

—Is there much pressure in your country for young men and women to get married? What is the stereotypical image of the 40-year-old single male? the 40-year-old single female? Are they the same or different?

St. Martin's

CAMBRIDGE
UNIVERSITY PRESS
ISBN 0-521-65767-9

9 780521 657679

LEKI

ISBN 0-312-09215-6